Grasshoppers

by Cheryl Coughlan

Consulting Editor: Gail Saunders-Smith, Ph.D.

Consultant: Gary A. Dunn, Director of Education,
Young Entomologists' Society

Pebble Books

an imprint of Capstone Press
Mankato, Minnesota

Pebble Books are published by Capstone Press
818 North Willow Street, Mankato, Minnesota 56001
http://www.capstone-press.com

Library of Congress Cataloging-in-Publication Data
Coughlan, Cheryl.
   Grasshoppers/by Cheryl Coughlan.
   p. cm.—(Insects)
   Includes bibliographical references (p. 23) and index.
   Summary: Simple text and photographs present the body parts and behavior
of grasshoppers.
   ISBN 0-7368-0241-X
   1. Grasshoppers—Juvenile literature. [1. Grasshoppers.] I. Title. II. Series:
Insects (Mankato, Minn.)
QL508.A2C735   1999
595.7′26—dc21   98-52815
                                                                                      CIP
                                                                                       AC

Note to Parents and Teachers

The Insects series supports national science standards for units on
the diversity and unity of life. The series shows that animals have
features that help them live in different environments. This book
describes and illustrates the parts of grasshoppers. The photographs
support early readers in understanding the text. The repetition of
words and phrases helps early readers learn new words. This book
also introduces early readers to subject-specific vocabulary words,
which are defined in the Words to Know section. Early readers may
need assistance to read some words and to use the Table of
Contents, Words to Know, Read More, Internet Sites, and
Index/Word List sections of the book.

Table of Contents

4

Most grasshoppers live
in grassy places.

6

Most grasshoppers are green or brown.

8

Grasshoppers have
a long body.

spiracles

Grasshoppers have
breathing holes
called spiracles.

Most grasshoppers have
four wings.

front legs

Grasshoppers have
short front legs.

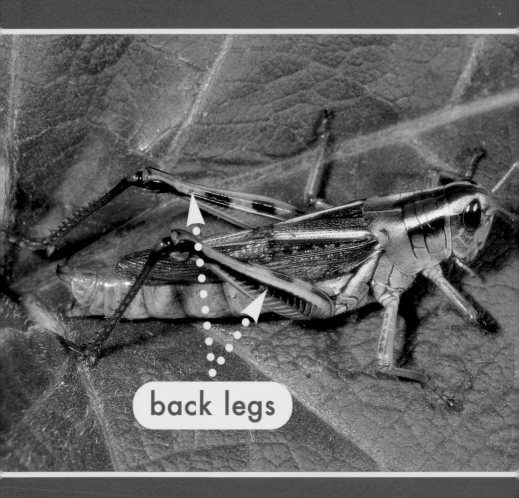

back legs

Grasshoppers have
long back legs.

18

Grasshoppers can jump far.

Grasshoppers use
brown spit to
keep away enemies.

Words to Know

enemy—a person or animal that wants to harm or destroy another; grasshopper enemies include birds, lizards, mice, monkeys, and snakes.

jump—to push off with the legs and feet and move through the air; grasshoppers can jump several times their own body length.

spiracles—holes on the sides of an insect's body that help it breathe; insects usually have from 9 to 11 pairs of spiracles.

wing—a movable part of an insect that helps it fly; most grasshoppers have four wings.

Read More

Gerholdt, James E. *Grasshoppers.* Incredible Insects. Edina, Minn.: Abdo & Daughters, 1996.

Kranking, Kathy. *The Bug Book.* New York: Golden Books, 1998.

Wilsdon, Christina. *National Audubon Society First Field Guide: Insects.* New York: Scholastic, 1998.

Internet Sites

Grasshoppers
http://www.connect.ab.ca/~bautista/insect/grass.htm

Grasshoppers: Expert High Jumpers
http://www.letsfindout.com/subjects/bug/rfijumpg.html

Insect Body Parts
http://www.uky.edu/Agriculture/Entomology/ythfacts/4h/unit1/labgrass.htm

Index/Word List

Word Count: 50
Early-Intervention Level: 8

Editorial Credits
Mari C. Schuh, editor; Timothy Halldin, cover designer; Kimberly Danger,
    photo researcher

Photo Credits
Bill Johnson, 20
David Liebman, cover, 1
Dwight R. Kuhn, 10, 16, 18
GeoIMAGERY/Fi Rust, 8
Lyle Quackenbush, 4
Michael Turco, 14
Root Resources/Earl L. Kubis, 6
Visuals Unlimited/Kjell B. Sandved, 12